IS
GOD
AT
HOME?

IS
GOD
AT
HOME?

J. B. Phillips

WIPF & STOCK · Eugene, Oregon

Wipf and Stock Publishers
199 W 8th Ave, Suite 3
Eugene, OR 97401

Is God at Home?
By Phillips, J. B.
Copyright©1957 SCM
ISBN 13: 978-1-62032-340-3
Publication date 7/1/2012
Previously published by Abingdon, 1957

Preface

EVERY CLERGYMAN, MINISTER, AND PASTOR WHO takes his work seriously is uncomfortably conscious of the gulf between the members of his church, who are frequently those with a Christian upbringing, and the ordinary people of the surrounding world. He knows that the Church in its preaching and in its writing is very often speaking to no more than its own members and hangers-on.

I believe I am not alone in believing that this unwilling insularity, this failure in communication, is due very largely to the failure of the Church to use the right language and thought-forms. Much language current in our churches is well understood by the churches' members (though sometimes all too unthinkingly accepted), but is nothing more nor less than technical jargon to men and women who for a generation or two have not been associated with any church. Such people naturally regard the Church and the Church's gospel as irrelevant when the language in which God's Word is spoken is almost completely divorced from the words and forms of thought of everyday experience.

Now the Christian who feels acutely the tragedy of this gulf between Church and people has two courses open to him. He may insist that it is perfectly right and proper that the Church should have its own language and expressions, and he may take the view that if people want to join the divine society, they must expect to take the trouble to learn the language. For myself I find serious objections to this point of view, for it is rare to find people so constrained to join the Church that they are willing to submit to instruction, as it were, before they can learn what the Church's message is.

The defenders of the jargon and phrases of the Church's traditions hold that there must of necessity be a specialized vocabulary, just as there is in any other specialized form of human activity, whether it is music, architecture, or electronic engineering. To me at least, this is a thoroughly unsound argument, for Christ did not come into the world to bring men "specialized activity," but life, fuller and more satisfying than it had ever

Preface

been before. If the churches have made Christianity appear to be some kind of specialized spiritual performance, so much the worse for them. The real purpose of Christ, the real relevance of the gospel, is surely to enable men to live together as sons of God. Human beings, like children, love to have secrets, love to be "in the know." But the Christian religion was never meant to be a secret recipe for living, held by a few. It is good news for all mankind; and, because it is that, the more clearly and intelligibly it can be presented, the more faithfully it is following its Master's purpose.

The second course open to the sensitive Christian is to try to learn the words and ways of thinking of the world by which he is surrounded. He must not be so proud that he will only read the most exclusive newspaper and the best-written books. He must not avert eyes of horror from the popular daily paper, from the current film success, or from the radio or television show which influences thinking in millions of homes. If a fisherman must study the habits of the fish he is to catch, it is surely not unreasonable to suggest that fishers of men should study the ways in which men think and feel and express themselves. We may hold in our hands the Word of life, but if we cannot communicate it to the people around us, it would almost be better if we did not hold it at all!

Like many others in the Christian ministry I have been concerned with this whole question of communication for several years. I know for a fact that many estimable Christian books never penetrate beyond a comparatively small circle of Christian readers. This is not in the least because the writers are out of sympathy with modern problems or out of touch with modern life, but simply because they have not learned the koine, the common language of today. It is significant to me as a translator that in the province of God the New Testament was written, not in the majestic and beautiful Greek of the classical period, but in the Greek of the market place and the port, the lingua franca of the then-known world. Surely there is a lesson to be learned from this simple fact. If we are going to be able to "communicate," many of us who have been educated and trained in theology will have to relearn the koine of today's world.

In this book there are collected together, in response to a number of requests, some attempts that have been made to communicate eternal

Preface

truths in the language of today. It is hoped that they will be found free from technical jargon, while faithfully expressing various facets of the Christian gospel. I am under no illusions as to their limitations and imperfections, but I hope that they will at least stimulate others to further efforts in the urgent modern art of communication.

J. B. PHILLIPS

Contents

1. IS GOD AT HOME? 15
2. ARE YOU A MAN OR A MOUSE?.. 20
3. RECIPE FOR HAPPINESS 23
4. IS GOD LIKE FATHER CHRISTMAS? 27
5. THE ROAD TO FREEDOM 31
6. TIME MARCHES ON 34
7. GOD AND THE COLLEGE DEGREE 37
8. I NEVER ASKED TO BE BORN 40
9. IT WALKS BY NIGHT 43

Is God at Home?

10. "MAY I TAKE IT TO THE LIGHT?" 46

11. HOW AM I DOING? 48

12. A WIZARD TYPE 51

13. THE COMFORT OF THE ATOM BOMB 54

14. I LIKE TO KEEP AN OPEN MIND.. 57

15. CHRISTMAS IS COMING 60

16. WHY GOOD FRIDAY? 63

17. THE FIRST EASTER PARADE 66

18. WHAT'S WHITSUN? 70

19. "BLOW THE BLUEPRINT!" 73

20. THE WAY TO LOVE 76

21. "MY PAST HAS CAUGHT UP WITH ME" 79

Contents

22. "NO! NO! A THOUSAND TIMES NO!" 82

23. HE'S WONDERFUL, ISN'T HE? 85

24. THE DUMB BLONDE 88

25. WHY SHOULD I SUPPORT THE CHURCH? 91

26. MEN UNDER RECONSTRUCTION 94

27. BE YOUR AGE, BROTHER! 97

28. WHY DON'T YOU RELAX? 100

29. HAVE YOU A SPLIT PERSONALITY? 103

30. IS GOD DEAD? 106

1

IS GOD AT HOME?

MOST PEOPLE BELIEVE IN SOME KIND OF GOD. It's quite difficult really to believe that all the wonders of the universe which science is gradually revealing to us were not designed by Someone.

But many people find it very hard to believe in God as a Person who is interested in the world and in the people to whom he has given life and the power to think. Terrible things happen in the world, like wars and concentration camps, and they can't help asking themselves, "Why doesn't God do something about it?" And then they see wicked people apparently getting away with their wickedness and decent-living people suffering quite undeservedly. So they conclude that although there probably is a God, he is a long way off and doesn't trouble to interfere with the problems of this planet. He may be "at home" in his own inaccessible heaven, but apparently he's not "at home" to us poor mortals who sometimes long for the reassurance that he cares about us.

In spite of all this, millions of people all over the world apparently do know God as a Person and find him a very great help to guide and inspire their lives. Some of them perhaps may be believing simply because they want to believe, and some of them may be believing in utterly blind faith— they haven't got the sort of minds which ask awkward questions! But all the same, there are crowds of people who have critical and inquiring minds, who have faced squarely the problems and tragedies of life, and who are yet convinced not only that there is a God but also that he is at home to us human beings.

Some people of course are looking for the wrong kind of God, the kind who doesn't make human beings at all but automatic creatures who are incapable of doing anything wrong. Some are still hoping vainly for a world that is run like a kindergarten, where good is immediately rewarded and evil is automatically checked or punished. Some feel a perpetual resentment against God because they picture him sitting comfortably on a throne somewhere up above while we men and women sweat and strive and suffer.

Now it is obviously very much more sensible to try to find out on what terms God is running this world than to make up the sort of terms we should like, and then feel bitter against God because he doesn't come up to our expectations! A little honest observation of life will soon show us that we've all been given the risky gift of free will. Man is free to choose, and when people complain that God doesn't stop the frightful horrors of war, for instance, they might equally well complain that he doesn't stop them from making uncharitable remarks or feeling bitter resentment. We are all free to commit evils if we want to, whether they are big or small.

The "good news" of the Christian faith is that although God is "at home" to every sincere seeker after truth, yet, if we may put it so, he did not stay at home. In order to show men how life should be lived, he entered into the life of this planet by being born and living a human life as Jesus. He—who was God, remember—did not enjoy any special privileges or protection. He

Is God at Home?

lived life and endured temptation in the same way that you and I have to live and endure it. What is more, when man's evil and hatred of truth closed round Jesus to kill him, there was no celestial rescue party. He simply went on to die a cruel and ignominious death. Then, to prove who it was who had visited the planet in person, he returned to life and showed himself plainly on dozens of occasions to reliable witnesses. These men were convinced, and they went out to tell the world that God is not some faraway, disinterested Power, but One who loves men so much that he himself entered into the train and muddle of human living to show men how to live and to bear in his own person the ultimate consequences of evil.

Now the millions referred to above who know and love God have come to know him through accepting the claims and teaching of the Man Jesus Christ. God becomes, not a vague and distant Power, but a Father well able to support and inspire us through our temporary life in this world, and willing to welcome us after what we call "death" into his heavenly home.

We may be looking in the wrong direction; we

Is God at Home?

may be expecting the wrong kind of God; but if we seriously want to find God for ourselves, we can be quite certain of finding him through his own revelation of himself in terms that we can understand—in other words, through believing with mind and heart in Jesus Christ.

2

ARE YOU A MAN OR A MOUSE?

EVERY YEAR IN THE HARVEST FIELDS OF ENGLAND there are thousands of little tragedies. The victims are those charming little creatures the harvest mice.

Earlier in the year the growing corn seems to them to be the ideal place in which to settle and bring up a family. Food, shelter, and building material are there in plenty, and everything seems perfectly adapted for their needs. The forest of innumerable cornstalks is their whole world, and in it they court and play, mate and bring up their families. Their happiness seems to be complete.

Until the harvest. For when the day comes for the owner of the field to reap his harvest, tragedy inevitably begins for the harvest mouse. The whole world of waving corn which seemed so snug and secure, so specially designed for his comfort and nourishment, comes crashing about his ears. The field which he thought was his world never really belonged to him at all, and the fact that the growing corn was not meant for his food and shelter has, alas, not entered his tiny head.

The life of the harvest mouse is not a bad picture of the way in which some people live in this world. They too work and play, court and get married and bring up children, in the happy belief that it is their world, and that to believe in an eventual "harvest" is old-fashioned and silly. Yet Jesus Christ, who claimed to be the Son of God, said quite plainly that this world is like a field that belongs to God and that it is moving inevitably toward a harvest. You can read his words about it in Matthew's Gospel, chapter 13, verses 24-43. For this little world is not, as some imagine, a permanent thing at all. When God decides that his great experiment has gone on long enough, he will reap the harvest. To quote Christ's words: "The harvest is the end of the world."

The field mouse is deceived because for months he is left to his own devices. He never sees the owner of the field and naturally knows nothing of the coming harvest. Many people allow themselves to be deceived because God, the Owner of the world, does not put in an appearance, and for the purposes of the experiment we call life he does not interfere with man's power to choose. Many of them imagine that the "field" belongs to man and that there is no such thing as an eventual "harvest."

But if Christ really was, as he claimed to be, God, then his statement about this world's being an experimental field with an inevitable harvest should surely be most seriously considered. No one could blame the little harvest mouse for not realizing the true purpose of the cornfield or the certainty of the eventual reaping. But what are we—mice or men?

3

RECIPE FOR HAPPINESS

THERE IS A RIGHT WAY TO DO EVERYTHING—AND usually dozens of wrong ones. If you have been muddling along, doing a job in any old way, what a relief it is to be shown by the expert how the thing really should be done. Not only do we save ourselves much wear and tear, but we feel much more satisfied when we have learned the right way, even though it may hurt our pride a bit to unlearn the method we were using before.

Christians believe that there is a right way of doing the most important job of all—*living*—and there are plenty of wrong ones. They believe that Jesus Christ, who claimed to be God living on this earth as Man, gave us the clue for the right way of living—what we might call the "recipe for happiness." It comes in what is often called the Sermon on the Mount, in Matthew's Gospel, chapter 5,

Is God at Home?

verses 3-9, and it is printed here just as it is in the Bible. It is a pretty revolutionary recipe, and in order to show up the contrast between what Christ said and what is commonly thought, the two points of view are printed one below the other. By the way, the old-fashioned word "blessed" really means "happy."

Most People Think

Blessed are the "pushers": for they get on in the world.

Blessed are the hard-boiled: for they never let life hurt them.

Blessed are they who complain: for they get their own way in the end.

Blessed are the blasé: for they never worry over their sins.

Blessed are the slave drivers: for they get results.

Blessed are the knowledgeable men of the world: for they know their way around.

Blessed are the troublemakers: for they make people take notice of them.

Jesus Christ Said

Blessed are the poor in spirit[1]: for theirs is the kingdom of heaven.

---

[1] Meaning humble, not what we mean by poor-spirited.

Recipe for Happiness

Blessed are they that mourn: for they shall be comforted.

Blessed are the meek[2]: for they shall inherit the earth.

Blessed are they which do hunger and thirst after righteousness: for they shall be filled.

Blessed are the merciful: for they shall obtain mercy.

Blessed are the pure in heart: for they shall see God.

Blessed are the peacemakers: for they shall be called the children of God.

A good many people are trying the first recipe, and the result is a world full of unhappiness, greed, cruelty, and selfishness. If, as Christians believe, the way that Jesus recommended is the right one, recommended by the expert in living, then that is not surprising.

The latter recipe may not look very attractive and it may not look as if it would work. But those who have taken the trouble to study it and put it into practice find that life lived according to that recipe is very happy and very satisfying, and

---

[2] Meaning those who accept life, not meek-and-mild. Jesus was meek but not mild.

makes them feel that this is the way life was meant to be lived.

To effect the change-over means a clear-cut decision—and adequate power to prevent your relapsing into the old way. The first is your concern; and you will find that God is well able to look after the second if you mean business.

4

IS GOD LIKE FATHER CHRISTMAS?

OF COURSE IF GOD IS REALLY SUCH AN EASY-GOING person as Father Christmas, there is no sense in Christianity at all. All the fuss about God's sending his Son into the world to die for our sins and bring us safe to heaven is much ado about nothing.

Yet it is at least possible that God is really highly dangerous. If he is absolute goodness and purity as well as absolute love, it is quite reasonable to suppose that in his immediate presence evil cannot live for a split second. A bright light destroys darkness, a blazing fire destroys cold, an antiseptic destroys germs, not because they are in a furious temper about it, but because it is their nature to do so. It is perfectly reasonable to suppose that God means instant death to every form of evil by reason of his very nature. And that is a pretty alarming thought.

This is really what all the "fuss" is about, and the question which every serious religion has to answer is this: "How can man, who knows very well that he is infected with evil, safely approach God's presence—to which he is being inevitably carried nearer, every day of his life?" The old-fashioned word "salvation" means simply the state of being made safe, and that is precisely what the Christian gospel offers. It means that imperfect and sinful man can exist safely in the blazing radiance of God's perfection. It means that he can safely regard God as his Friend and heaven as his home.

The method God chose to make this salvation possible was briefly this: He came personally to this world some nineteen hundred years ago by being born into it as a human baby, and he was known as Jesus Christ. He lived over thirty years of successful resistance against the forces of evil (which naturally made the most of this unique opportunity!); he did a great deal of good and taught people unforgettable facts about themselves and about God. Then he deliberately allowed the forces of evil to close in upon him and kill him. It is as though he said: "I, though I am God, am also Representative Man. I am sinless, but I am going to allow evil to run its inevitable course in my own person—and that will naturally mean death." (It is impossible for us to imagine the courage involved here, because we cannot really conceive the frightful repulsion that God must feel in allowing evil actually to touch and kill him.)

So he died. It looked a bit like a martyr's death, but it wasn't. It was the Representative Man paying the price of mankind's evil, which is always, sooner or later, death. What makes it such a unique and important happening is that the Representative Man was in fact God himself.

So great was the vitality of the Man who had never sinned that death had nothing with which to hold him. Within three days he was demonstrating the fact that he was alive, in broad daylight and in the open air, not once but again and again!

And here is the gospel, or good news. Before Christ returned to resume his position as God, he instructed his followers to tell the world that any mortal man who turned from his self-centered way of living and honestly entrusted his life to him, could freely and fearlessly approach God as his

Father, and could look forward without misgiving to heaven as his ultimate home.

We can choose—either the imaginary God like Father Christmas, or the real God, who has personally, at great cost, made it possible for us to be safe and at home in his presence.

5

THE ROAD TO FREEDOM

THERE IS A LOT OF TALK TODAY, AND THERE ALways has been a lot of talk, about freedom. Most people long to be free, but precious few of them are. Circumstances, politics, economics, even religion, all get blamed. "If only I were really free to do just what I like" is the secret, but very common, dream of many hearts.

But does real freedom mean that you (and all the others, of course) are to be free to do exactly what you like? A man may say he has no use for rules and regulations, and determine to be free. He therefore disregards, for instance, the traffic laws. But if he's a motorist, he soon finds that he does not in fact find freedom, but a crash, or a fine, or both.

The man who can't be bothered with rules, in playing tennis, for instance, and persists in calling

Is God at Home?

his smashing service "in" when it's really "out," very soon finds that he's not free to play tennis at all—at any rate with normal people. He isn't anything like so free as the expert who has spent years not only in mastering the rules, but in learning the complex technique of the really first-class player.

The same applies to any sport and any decent job of work; the conceited fellow who won't learn is never free to do the thing properly. It is the man who has the sense to come down to earth and learn the rules and technique who finds that he becomes more and more free to function, whatever the activity of mind or body may be.

Life is like that. People whose main concern is to despise all rules and do exactly what they like never succeed in being really free. Like the half-witted imaginary motorist mentioned above, they refuse even to recognize any laws. Sooner or later they crash, and, unfortunately, they're not the only ones to get hurt. Whether it's in matters of sex or money or anything else, they're "free," they say, and when the crash against the invisible rules of life comes, they'll blame anything—luck, or other people, or even God, but never themselves.

Christ said, among other things, that he came to make men free. He taught not only that there

The Road to Freedom

are certain unseen laws behind life which can't be safely ignored, but also that there is a new technique of living by which men learn to be free. Those who have taken the trouble to learn this say that he was right. They find they're free to be and do what in their secret hearts they had always hoped that they were capable of being and doing. They find this is real freedom, whatever the external circumstances may be.

Of course you can ignore the rules and refuse to learn the technique till your dying day—no one will stop you. But you won't find freedom—only frustration and that ridiculous infantile wish at the back of your mind, "Oh, I do wish I could be free to do what I like!"

6

TIME MARCHES ON

Time marches on! And the world, some people tell us, is gradually getting better. True, it is still full of pain and sorrow, greed and injustice, but all these miseries are only to be looked upon as the "growing pains of civilization." It may take millions of years, but the onward progress of the human race is inevitable, and in the end science will conquer all pain and disease, scientific planning will solve all economic difficulties, and psychology will disentangle all problems of personality. And of course all the childish belief in God and heaven and hell will just quietly die out. Life will be so splendid that there will be no need to invent a heaven above the bright blue sky.

All this will take time, and you and I will have been dead and gone long ago. But we mustn't mind that, for all our struggles, all the pains we bear, will all be part of the price that must be paid for the eventual happiness of our great-great-great-great-

Time Marches On

great-great- (and possibly a few more) grandchildren. These distant descendants of ours will have, it seems, a perfectly marvelous time.

But time marches on, and what is going to happen when the above goal is reached? Well, most scientists agree that the life of the human race on this planet can only be for a limited time, perhaps a few million years. After that the sun's vast energy will have been exhausted so much that life can no longer be sustained on this planet. It will not, of course, happen suddenly, but ultimately the world will become as cold and airless and dead as the moon.

This means that supposing this marvelous progress of the human race really takes place, and future generations are incredibly healthy, wealthy, and wise, yet the end will be silence, cold, and death. Think of it; the whole process which has lasted millions of years, the whole sum of human struggles, endeavors, hopes, and fears will end in the deathly cold of interstellar space! What a prospect! What an ideal for which to live and work and die!

The Christian religion, of course, has always taught something quite different. According to its Founder, Jesus Christ, this life is only a temporary

Is God at Home?

and limited preface to real life—i.e., sharing the life of God beyond the limitations of time and space. The Christian, while he lives in this world, does his best to make it better, to relieve suffering, to right wrongs and spread happiness and the joy that he has discovered in knowing God. Even here and now he has begun to taste something of the flavor of the real and permanent life of God, but his eventual goal does not belong to this little planet at all. This is only the testing ground, and it doesn't particularly matter whether it lasts ten years or ten million. Real living, real beauty, real knowledge, all these things and thousands more are waiting for him as he blossoms out into his full development in God's perfect world, sometimes called heaven.

If you are interested in this very satisfying and sensible way of looking at life, and are a little tired of being assured of the inevitability of human progress, a very good start may be made by reading what is called the Gospel of John. Here you can read of the doings and sayings of a man who claimed to be the Son of God, and who consequently spoke with considerable authority. You may find, as many have, that what he said has the ring of truth.

7

GOD AND THE COLLEGE DEGREE

THE COLLEGE OR UNIVERSITY DEGREE IS A RECOGnized standard of achievement. Every year thousands of students all over the world work hard to pass the examination, because they know that the degree they are working for will be accepted as a recognized standard.

Most people never stop to think that the reason why a college or university degree is so accepted is simply because the learning and reputation of the college or university lie behind the granting of it. If the educational authority were proved to be fraudulent or in some way bogus, the value of the degree would fall to zero at once. The student might put in just as much work, he might even sit for the examination, but if it were suddenly re-

Is God at Home?

vealed that the university was a phony one, the value of his achievement would be nil.

This is of course a fantastic idea, but is it any more fantastic than the common practice of many people, who try to lead good lives without any belief in the existence of God? Just as the exam has no value without the university, so "good" is meaningless unless there is a supreme Power of good. If there is in fact no God, I may call your good "evil" and you may do the same for me—and who is to say which of us is right? Without God there is no standard. You may consider the Communist philosophy of life brutal and degrading, but the Communist may retort that your way of life seems to him to be weak and sentimental. Without God it remains a mere matter of opinion.

The Christian religion stoutly maintains that there can be no real standards of conduct for either men or nations without a real belief in God. Moreover these standards are not mere vague ideals, but actual rules for living; and Christians believe that God gave men these rules for happy and constructive living when he visited this planet nineteen hundred years ago. You can read for yourself what

God and the College Degree

he had to say, in the first part of what is now called the New Testament.

If you accept what he said, you find yourself no longer like a student working for a doubtful university, but a co-operator with the Power behind this immensely complex world.

8

I NEVER ASKED TO BE BORN

OF COURSE YOU DIDN'T—NOBODY EVER DID! BUT people make this sort of remark usually when they've made a bit of a mess of things or when life isn't working out to their own liking. They wash their hands of all responsibility—"*I* didn't make my own nature and temperament, *I* wouldn't have designed life like this at all, in fact I never asked to be born!"

We know in our best moments that talking like this is waste of breath. When you start thinking seriously about it, life and being alive at all are a very great mystery. While you are reading these words, you are using eyes that you never designed, at the same time breathing with lungs that you had no hand in making, and simultaneously digesting your last meal by an extremely involved process that you probably know very little about. In fact you yourself are living in a highly complex machine which we call the human body, and you had no part at all in the planning of it.

This attitude of absolving ourselves from all responsibility in the matter doesn't really lead anywhere, and it most certainly doesn't bring us happiness. All we know is that some mysterious Power has given us life and personality and certain gifts. It is therefore much more sensible to try to find out what is the plan behind the mysterious Power than grumble because life doesn't bring us all we want.

Well, we could spend a lifetime guessing what this Power is up to, what it, or he, is trying to do, and if there's any sense in it anyway. An alternative, which many people have found highly satisfying, is to accept one supreme fact of history: that the Power behind the universe did at a particular point in time enter the life of this planet as a human being. He did this partly to show men what sort of Person he is in a way that they could understand, and partly to show them what his plan for life on this planet really is.

Jesus Christ is the Man who made this astounding claim. He *did* "ask to be born," so to speak, for he came into this world deliberately and he willingly and cheerfully accepted life—and death. It is therefore very worth while reading in the New Testament what he said and did and claimed to be. He did not answer every question or tell us *why* we are here, but he did outline the plan for happy, satisfying life. Those who accept his claim and his teaching find that it makes sense in practice, and you don't ever find them complaining, "I never asked to be born!"

9

IT WALKS BY NIGHT

NIGHT SEEMS TO BE THE USUAL TIME FOR GHOSTS to walk. You don't often hear of anyone's seeing a ghost on a blazing summer afternoon; the spirits seem to prefer the shadows of the night. Perhaps that's because people can't be quite sure what they do see then, and fatigue has made them rather more susceptible to suggestion. Besides, most of us give our imaginations a little play in the evenings and keep our matter-of-factness for working hours.

Maybe that explains why we never hear of a séance being held in bright sunshine in the open air. Mediums say they must have the right "atmosphere," and that usually means a darkened room, a ring of clasped hands, and not too much skepticism present; otherwise the spirits can't get through.

All this makes it all the more remarkable that

Is God at Home?

when a man did come back from the dead, it was all so free from "spookiness," and most of the action took place in daylight in the open air. But perhaps he did it deliberately, just to show that this was the real thing.

There was no doubt that he really died, for it was all horribly visible—a public execution on a trumped-up charge. Yet within a few days he showed himself to be really and truly alive not once but several times. His friends who from a safe distance had seen him executed were certainly not expecting ever to see him alive again. Indeed they were most skeptical when the first report of his being alive came in. "Hysterical female nonsense!" they considered it. But when they saw him, not in the half-dark where they might have been mistaken for a moment, but in broad daylight, all they could say then was, "It must be a ghost!" And, to put it bluntly, they yelled with sheer fright.

We can't exactly blame them. It's one thing to see a white shape in a churchyard at night (which might after all be merely a cat), but it's quite a different matter when a friend whom you saw die on Friday comes up and speaks to you on the following Sunday morning! Yet this is what happened to the followers of Jesus Christ. He understood their fear, of course. He made them touch him and handle him to prove that he was really there, and then, when they still seemed a little slow in the uptake, he ate some food, for who ever heard of a ghost making a hearty meal? He had said he would conquer death, and here he was alive and well to prove it.

Of course it shook them. They'd been inclined for some time to believe his claim to be God walking the earth in human form, but this clinched it. Now they *knew*, and it wasn't long before they were out telling the world about him, and nothing on earth could stop them.

What changed these very ordinary men (who were such cowards that they didn't dare stand too near the cross in case they got involved) into heroes who would stop at nothing? A swindle? Hallucination? Spooky nonsense in a darkened room? Or Somebody quietly doing what he said he'd do— walk right through death?

What do *you* think?

10

"MAY I TAKE IT TO THE LIGHT?"

THINGS LOOK DIFFERENT IN DIFFERENT LIGHTS. The prettiest girl, with her hair and face and whole color scheme just right, looks frightful if you see her under the mercury-vapor lights of some of our main roads. Deathlike pallor, purple lips, and all her carefully chosen colors looking ghastly—just because you're seeing her in the wrong light.

On the other hand, soft rosy lights have a habit of making things, and people, rather more romantic than they really are. And sometimes we get taken in by seeing things in the wrong light. Daylight is the best test—which is why we often say in the clothing shop: "May I take it to the light?"

The same thing is true metaphorically. "In the light of my experience," we say, or "in the light of present-day knowledge." In fact there are so many different lights in which things can be seen and judged that some people say that nothing is *really* right or wrong—it just depends on the light in which you see it. This means logically that the burglar who makes a valuable haul has done something good and successful according to the light in which he sees his action, but the unfortunate householder sees the same thing as a disaster because, naturally enough, he sees it in a different light!

Isn't there a real light, a sort of Daylight, by which actions can be properly judged?

Well, there was a Man once who claimed to be himself the world's Light, meaning that in his character and teaching and actions men could find a sort of genuine daylight by which good and evil and different courses of actions could be judged. Of course, he got into serious trouble for making such a claim, though no one was actually able to prove him wrong, and in the end he was sentenced to death for claiming to be God.

All the same a lot of people believed he was right, and quite a good many do so today. His name is Jesus Christ.

11

HOW AM I DOING?

When we learn to do something new, like ice skating or driving a car, it isn't long before we ask the kind friend who is teaching us, about our progress. "How am I doing?" we say.

In the larger business of living perhaps we don't very often ask other people's opinion as to how we are getting on, though we all did when we were children. Probably we feel that we have enough experience and judgment to know for ourselves just "how we are doing." If we are confident and reasonably happy, and doing pretty well compared with our fellows, we don't bother very much about it. We just sometimes say to ourselves: "You're doing all right." Of course if we are secretly feeling a bit inferior, though we would never admit it, we may find ourselves trying to find out what other people think of us and our

How Am I Doing?

progress. We don't actually ask: "How am I doing?" but that is what we really want to know!

For to most people, whatever they may say to the contrary, it is a matter of great importance that they should stand well either in their own eyes or in those of other people, or both. But how very few people ever bother to think about how they are doing in the eyes of the Power behind everything, the One whom we call God! Yet if it is true that this is his world, and that he has laid down certain rules and principles for happy and constructive living, surely it is important to pay some attention to his standards—particularly if we hope one day, when our bodies die, to live permanently in his perfect world. There is a neat little story in the New Testament which has something to say on this point. It is in Luke's Gospel, chapter 12, verses 16-21.

For after all, even the most self-satisfied people sometimes ask themselves such questions as: "What am I here for?" "What sort of person am I meant to be?" "What sort of standards ought I to live by, and where shall I find them?" If we ask ourselves questions like these, we are really asking: "How am I doing?"—not by my own standards or those of my friends but by the permanent standards of

Is God at Home?

the One behind the universe—and that is a very important question indeed.

For if, as Christians believe, God is not a vague absentee Power but One who has shown men his standards and requirements by personally visiting this planet, isn't it only common sense to see what they are? The first part of the New Testament, called "the Gospels," is a plain, unvarnished account of what God said and did during his personal visit to the earth some nineteen hundred years ago, and it is written by those who were actual eyewitnesses of this extraordinary event, though they hardly knew what was happening at the time.

The world is in a frightful muddle, that is obviously true. Isn't it at least possible that this is because so many people are setting their standards of behavior either by their own judgment or by that of their neighbors, and so very few are even trying to follow the way of life that God demonstrated and taught when he visited the earth as the Man Jesus Christ?

12

A WIZARD TYPE

ARE PEOPLE JUST TYPES—GOOD, BAD, OR INDIFferent types?

Quite a lot of people think so. They think that what men and women are depends a bit on heredity and upbringing, etc., but chiefly on the type of temperament and character that the unseen glands in their bodies produce. If the glands are doing their stuff, then you get your cheery, confident, energetic type. But if they're not doing so well, then you get the poor, miserable sort of type, possibly with some sort of kink.

Since at present science can't alter the action of these glands very much, it seems that people are bound to become and remain their particular type —which is very nice if you're lucky enough to be a good type, but just too bad if you happen to be a bad type.

Is God at Home?

And, of course, if it's really true that people will always conform to type and no power on earth can alter them, then it's a pretty grim lookout for the world, for you can't improve the world if there's no way of changing the people who live in it.

The Christian religion has always taken a dim view of this pessimistic way of thinking. It claims that human nature *can* be changed, and it has proved that even the poorest types can rise to amazing heights of usefulness and courage. But let us be quite clear about what it does not claim. There is a certain amount of truth in this "type" business, and no amount of Christian faith is going to produce in us a good ear for music or a good head for figures, for example, if we haven't got these things already. But a real faith in Jesus Christ can and will alter the inner direction of our lives—it will change what we set our hearts on and "save" us from the hell of self-centered living. This can happen to us no matter what type we may be.

And what exactly do we mean by this "real faith in Jesus Christ"? Well, it means accepting, after fair consideration, the claim of Jesus Christ to be God visiting this earth in person as a Man. Accepting this gives us a lot—definite standards of living, facts about the character of God and the

A Wizard Type

ways in which he works. It also means a call to all that is in us to help build a Kingdom based on inner loyalty to the Power behind the whole vast concern. We find when we answer this call that a new spirit begins to develop inside our own personalities, as though God were giving us a bit of his own heredity.

How completely different the world would be if all the different types had this common loyalty and something of this new spirit! This is what Christians have been trying to spread for nineteen centuries. Maybe they haven't done it very well, but they've done enough to show the possibilities —for all types. Do you want to help, or hinder?

13

THE COMFORT OF THE ATOM BOMB

IT IS A COMMONPLACE TO SAY THAT THE WHOLE civilized world has been profoundly shocked at the fearful powers of destruction that science has put into men's hands by the discovery of the atomic bomb. But the way in which this has made even the most thoughtless realize what sort of world this is in which we live, is a very good thing. For years the materialist has been saying that the only "real" things are those which can be weighed and measured, seen and touched, and that all the spiritual things which are taught by true religion are vague, shadowy, and "unreal." But now the boot is on the other foot, and materialism has received a deathblow.

Everybody who reads a newspaper now knows that all the things that seem so solid and hard and

The Comfort of the Atom Bomb

permanent are not really so at all. They seem solid only because the particles that compose the atoms of which everything is composed are moving round the central "nucleus" at such a fantastic speed. Once loose those particles, as is done in the atomic bomb, and the most solid things that we know, like steel and concrete, are less substantial than a puff of cigarette smoke.

It is surely a comfort to know that people are beginning to see that the "real" things are the spiritual. No atomic bomb, however powerful, could destroy, for example, love or faith or hope or courage or self-sacrifice, any more than you can cut a sunbeam to pieces with a sword. The qualities which cannot be bought or sold, which cannot be measured or weighed or seen or handled, they are the permanent, indestructible things. It is the material world which is impermanent and unsubstantial. The body can be blown to pieces, but not the spirit.

This is, of course, what the Bible has been saying for centuries. It has pointed out that this present setup that we call life is only temporary, and that man is not merely a physical and mental phenomenon but a spiritual being. He is not therefore to be taken in or overwhelmed by either the glamours or the accidents of this life, but to concentrate upon establishing and maintaining his real —that is, spiritual—life. The Bible tells him how to do this, and shows how it is perfectly possible for anyone to be rescued from the inevitable disintegration of the merely material world and firmly established in the permanent world. When this has happened to a man, he has nothing to fear from this world, and death itself can only mean the casting off of the temporary and imperfect.

Here are some passages in the New Testament which may usefully be referred to:

John's Gospel, chapter 3, verses 1-21; the eighth chapter of Paul's Letter to the Romans; the third chapter of Peter's Second Letter; the fourth chapter of the First Letter of John.

There is comfort, then, in this new discovery. It has provided an unanswerable demonstration that materialism is not enough, and an endorsement of the hope that lies deep in every man's heart— that he is not merely a creature of a few years' life on this planet, but made to share the eternal life of God. The New Testament shows how this hope can come true for everyone who is ready to believe its message.

14

I LIKE TO KEEP AN OPEN MIND

YES, IT'S A FINE THING TO HAVE AN OPEN MIND—if it means you're willing to hear both sides of a question, and then *make up* your mind!

But sometimes when people say they like to "keep an open mind," they mean something rather different. They mean they want to save themselves the trouble of making a decision or bearing any responsibility which that might bring.

Take God, for instance. Crowds of people say they like to keep an open mind about God and religion and all that sort of thing, but most of them mean they aren't really going to decide about Christianity one way or the other. If they really meant they were keeping an open mind, you'd find them studying how the Christian religion began and its influence on the course of human

Is God at Home?

history, etc., not just looking for the cranks and hypocrites that you might find in any movement.

Of course a lot of people claim that you've got to have an open mind where religion is concerned. They claim to be "agnostics," which is an old Greek word which means you just can't know—in other words, your guess is as good as mine!

But is that really true? Jesus Christ, who made the altogether astounding claim to be God in human form, once said that you can actually *know* whether his teaching is true or not. "If a man is willing to follow God the Father's plan," he said, "he will *know* whether my teaching is really true or just man-man stuff." (John 7:17.)

It's a bit hard, isn't it? So long as you keep an open mind, so long as you refuse to commit yourself, you just can't know, but the moment you are willing to live life according to the plan of living that Jesus Christ said was God's way for men to live, you *do* know! Something inside you tells you that this is the way life was meant to be lived; it feels right and happy and as though it were getting you somewhere.

That's why the Christian, without meaning to be, is often so infuriating to the man with the open mind. For all his faults and failures, the Christian

I Like to Keep an Open Mind

knows, now he has committed himself, that he is on the right track; while the man with the open mind doesn't really know why he's here or where he's going or even what life's all about. You can hardly blame him for being so annoyed that the Christian is so sure that his way is the right one, can you?

Keep an open mind, never make a decision about Jesus Christ, and you'll never be really sure of anything all your life. But once you've made up your mind about him, you'll be one of the people who know what they are doing, the followers of Jesus Christ.

15

CHRISTMAS IS COMING

"Christmas comes but once a year, and when it comes it brings good cheer." So says the old rhyme, and naturally everyone tries at Christmastime to enjoy as much good cheer as he can. But not everyone realizes the true and extraordinary story that lies behind Christmas. We may have a vague impression at the back of our minds of shepherds and angels and a star—like some kind of half-remembered fairy story of childhood, and with the passing of the years it has all become very beautiful and romantic.

Yet in reality, although it is a most wonderful fact of history, it was not at the time particularly beautiful. For when God decided to enter the stream of human history by becoming a human baby, he did not choose, as we might expect, to be born in a rich and privileged home. There were no priorities or special advantages for him. He chose as his mother a peasant woman in humble circumstances.

There was no publicity and no fuss when he slipped like this into human life. It happened in a third-rate country some nineteen hundred years ago, and very few people knew what was happening. It may look beautiful now on a Christmas card or in a religious picture, but there is not really anything lovely in hunting desperately for lodgings when your wife is pregnant and near her time. There is nothing romantic in having your first baby in a drafty cave because no one in the inn next door will give up his bed for you, and it isn't really much fun to put your baby to sleep in the cattle's feeding trough because there is nowhere else except the dirty floor. The historic fact, shorn of its romance and decoration, was rather ugly and squalid. It is not a pleasant thing for a mother to feel that the world has no room for her baby.

How it must have cheered Mary when the rough shepherds came bursting in, all breathless and excited, saying that they had had a vision of angels up there on the hillside and had been told that this little fellow was really God, and might they please kneel and give him their presents! How the people snoring comfortably in the inn next door would have laughed to have seen the sight of those country bumpkins kneeling on the stable floor! It would have been as good as a play!

Yet that is how God made his entrance. If you can once imagine the contrast between the splendors of heaven and the squalors of earth, you cannot help admiring and loving a character who accepted no special advantages or defenses, who lived life on the same terms as his creatures. That is the real good cheer of Christmas: that God is not an aloof Invisible Power, but One who actually took the risk of entering his own world.

Cutting out the sentimentality, the decorations, and the commercial racket of Christmastime, the historic fact that we are celebrating is simple, but quite unforgettable once it gets under your skin. *God became one of us that we might find the way to become something like him.*

16

WHY GOOD FRIDAY?

MOST PEOPLE KNOW THAT THE EVENT COMMEMOrated every Good Friday was not a very pleasant affair. It was the death—it could be called the judicial murder—of a fine, courageous young man who dared to speak the truth. His name was Jesus, of Nazareth in Palestine, and you might say that what came to him was only what has been the fate of many other good men who have been tactless, or courageous, enough to speak the truth "never mind what."

Why then commemorate this particular little tragedy for nineteen hundred years, and why on earth call it *Good* Friday?

The answer depends on what, or who, you think Jesus Christ really was. If he was only another martyr to the truth, then that's that, and this long-drawn-out commemoration is a bit of a farce.

But if by any chance you take seriously his own

Is God at Home?

claim to be God—God "scaled down" of course to match this planet, but none the less genuinely God and a real human being at the same time—then you can't regard it as a nasty little incident that happened ages ago; it is something to make the least sensitive think twice.

It is an amazing situation, if true. God decides to exhibit his character in a way that men can understand by a personal visit to this planet that he has made. When he does so, a few recognize him, after a time, for what he is. A few more realize that what he tells them about God and man and life and all the other really important things has the ring of truth—he sounds like an expert speaking on his own subject. A good many more don't care much one way or the other, while a few bitterly resent his exposure of their pride and greed and hypocrisy. He is "the real thing"; they are not, and they know it. Consequently they become so blinded with fury that they engineer his death.

They succeed. They manage to get the Man who claimed to be God killed. Nothing exciting happens; there is no celestial rescue party at the last moment. After suffering agony, he dies.

It rather changes your view of God if you believe he experienced this. Conscience sometimes

Why Good Friday?

paints him as an angry Judge, and to a good many people he remains a shadowy, remote power apparently indifferent to this world's sufferings. But suppose this claim of Christ was true. Suppose that God did become man, Representative Man, so to speak; and that he allowed himself to become the target of evil, to suffer and die for man's sake. It's difficult to hate a God like that, and it's difficult to like any form of evil once you see its objective exposed as it was then. Its real desire is plainly to kill truth and goodness—and God too if he puts himself in a vulnerable position!

Those who think God did this almost incredible thing call it Good Friday because only an extremely good God could do a thing like that. All religions attempt to bridge the gulf between the terrific purity of God and the sinfulness of man, but Christianity believes that God built the bridge himself. This particular Friday commemorates his deliberate action in allowing himself to be caught up in the sin-suffering-death mechanism which haunts mankind.

He didn't let it end there, for he went on, right through death. But the men who believe in him can't forget the kind of Person such an act reveals. That's why they call it *Good* Friday.

17

THE FIRST EASTER PARADE

EASTER ISN'T JUST A HOLIDAY. IT'S NOT MERELY A convenient week end to mark the end of winter and the beginning of spring. It is, and has been for a very long time, the commemoration of a certain fact of history so remarkable that if it had happened today, all the newspapers would be full of it!

What happened (and the event was well authenticated by eyewitnesses at the time) was that a man became alive again after he had died. There wasn't any doubt about the fact of his death, for his enemies, who didn't care for his plain speaking or his character, engineered his death on political grounds—what we should call today a "judicial murder." This was all quite public, so that a lot of people saw him die.

The First Easter Parade

It therefore came as a terrific shock to his friends and followers to find that, as he had promised, he could and did walk right through death. Imagine your own feelings if you had been to a friend's funeral on Good Friday, and then found him in your own dining room alive and well on the following Sunday, cheerfully wishing you a happy Easter! It would shake you. It certainly shook those men and women who first saw this actual demonstration, this parade of Life conquering Death. They were scared stiff, and can you blame them?

Of course they thought he must be a ghost or an "appearance" or something. That he was really alive just couldn't *be!* He had to make them touch him, he had to eat a meal in front of them, he had to use his own familiar gestures before they could believe it really had happened.

Then it dawned. *It was true!* This man, the finest and best they'd ever known, the one who had told them how life ought to be lived and told them what sort of Person God was, had in fact come through all the ghastly business of crucifixion and done what he had calmly told them he would do—conquer death. They remembered then various strange things he had said—about himself being God in human form and at the same time

Is God at Home?

being, so to speak, Representative Man, and that his death would be the measure of God's love for men. If he had died and stayed dead, he would still have been a good man, but he would have been profoundly mistaken, and even a little strange in the head on certain subjects. *But he hadn't stayed dead!* In a flash they saw that the demonstration had proved to the hilt the truth of all his claims! It was the first Easter Parade, the Parade of the power of God over the evil power of death.

To say that these people were thrilled and inspired is to put it very mildly. After a demonstration like that they were ablaze with this new certainty, and no power on earth was going to stop them from telling the world. Men must and should be told what a magnificent Person God is, they must and should be told that he had shown men by practical demonstration that he loved them enough to go through death for them, and best of all had paraded death, the last and worst enemy, as conquered and liquidated. Any human life honestly committed to the Man who was also God could also pass through death—they had his word for that.

The man, of course, was Jesus Christ, and the story of what he did and was is plain for anyone

The First Easter Parade

to read in the New Testament. But it is very far from being an old dead story with the dust of the centuries thick upon it. Anybody who opens his personality to that Man will find that he is alive today. He can still transform a man's whole life, he can still give not only the directions for real living but the power to live, and he can still give that undefeatable certainty that death has been publicly defeated. The man whose life is sincerely entrusted to Christ can pass through death without a tremor.

18

WHAT'S WHITSUN?

WHAT IS WHITSUN, BESIDES BEING A BANK HOLIday?

Some people may have some half-remembered ideas from Sunday-school days of something rather queer happening on a day called Pentecost a long time ago. Weren't the Apostles, according to the story, supposed to speak in all kinds of languages at once, and wasn't there a lot of religious excitement? Is that what is being commemorated by the Church at Whitsun? And if it is, what has it got to do with us today?

Can we start again, and try to see if there isn't a good reason for remembering Whitsuntide? Here is a brief "recap."

Christmas, according to Christianity, is the anniversary of that almost incredible Act of God —his entering the stream of human life by be-

What's Whitsun?

coming a baby. Good Friday is the anniversary of the death of the Man that baby became, and it is called good because through that apparent tragedy God reconciled man to Himself.

Easter commemorates the historic fact that Jesus Christ conquered death and "came back" to show in a series of unmistakable demonstrations that he had really done so.

Whitsun follows on, and is the commemoration of a special occasion on which God did, with special emphasis, something that he is always prepared to do—that is, to give some of his own personality to those who are willing to receive him. It is therefore the birthday of the new community of men and women who joined together to achieve God's purposes by the power of his Spirit. It is the beginning of the Christian Church.

Without God's inner reinforcement Christianity remains a beautiful ideal—which no one can live up to. Man may admire the character of Christ, may see that his way of living is the right one, and may even try to follow him. But unless God can implant the moral power *inside,* the vision of being a Christian soon fades and becomes just another discarded ideal.

Now Christianity isn't meant to be a beautiful

Is God at Home?

ideal which no one can live out in practice. It is the way of real, happy constructive living. It is living in harmony with God, and with our fellow men. But because of the selfishness and evil around us (*and* in us) we find ourselves too weak, too cowardly, and too tied by past ways of thinking and feeling to embark on this real living.

This is where God comes in. To anyone who means business and sincerely wants to live life in the new way, God is prepared to give the inner reinforcement of his own Spirit. Fear and evil and selfishness are slowly but surely displaced by love, true goodness, and a willingness to live for God and other people.

This inward change-over, this strengthening of men's personalities by God's own personality, is what is being commemorated at Whitsun. On the first Whitsunday the early followers of Jesus Christ experienced an unforgettable demonstration that God could and would change and empower them to live for him. The "Acts of the Apostles" shows that it was no mere flash in the pan.

God hasn't changed. The same Spirit is instantly available wherever and whenever a man realizes his own moral weakness and genuinely opens his personality to receive his God.

19

"BLOW THE BLUEPRINT!"

"Look at the mess the world's in! Think of the pain and misery in millions of lives, and the fear and insecurity all round.... And then tell me there's a God of love!"

Don't make me laugh—or is it cry?

All right. But just suppose for a moment that all the workers on a building site said: "Blow the blueprint! Every man for himself, let's work out our own ideas!" When you saw the finished house (if it ever was finished), you'd say: "Tell me there's a designer behind all this? Don't make me laugh!"

That is what has happened in the world for a good many centuries, and it is still happening—hence the mess.

What proportion of all the people in the world, do you suppose, are following the Designer's blue-

Is God at Home?

print? A pretty small number. Many, of course, don't know about it, many don't bother to consult it, and a lot of people prefer their own ideas.

If the result is pretty chaotic, can you fairly blame the Designer?

Well, where is this master blueprint, this design for human living?

It's to be found in the New Testament. There we can read of a God who broke through from the real and permanent world into this life of time and space by becoming a Man. He was thus able not only to give men the blueprint for living but to live it out in person. In fact, you might say that he personally was the blueprint. And it becomes pretty plain as you read that if only men would live according to *that* design, the world would quickly recover and become an infinitely better and happier place.

If only! But men don't bother to read the plan. They don't give it the concentration they give to football scores or crossword puzzles. Maybe they find it difficult and give it up, or they're not prepared to abandon their own little plans. "Blow the blueprint!"

And so the world gets driven into a corner, a nasty, dangerous corner, and there's no way out

"Blow the Blueprint!"

except by people's scrapping their own selfish plans and trying to follow the master plan.

At present there is only a mere handful who have studied the plan and are trying to co-operate with the Designer.

What about you?

Do you say, "Blow the blueprint!" . . . and then try to shift the blame for all the mess on God, the Designer?

20

THE WAY TO LOVE

LOVE IS A MOST EXTRAORDINARY WORD—WE USE IT to mean so many things. It can mean the highest emotion of which a man or woman is capable, and yet we use the same word to describe quite trivial sentiments. People say for example: "I *love* chocolates with hard centers," or "I *love* sitting by the fire on a cold winter's night." Yet we probably all recognize that love, real love, is the biggest thing in the world.

Many years ago that great Christian Paul wrote a definition of the highest sort of love, the sort that is not self-centered but expresses itself constructively and unselfishly. His words can be found in any Bible, in the thirteenth chapter of the First Epistle to the Corinthians. They are printed here just as they are in the Bible, except that the word "love" has been substituted for the word "charity," because "charity" has come to mean something different from what it did when our English version of the Bible was written.

Below it is printed a definition of the opposite of Christian love, which is not hatred, as you might suppose, but love turned in upon itself—what is sometimes called self-love. The two definitions make a pretty effective contrast.

Love

Love suffereth long, and is kind; love envieth not; love vaunteth not itself, is not puffed up, doth not behave itself unseemly, seeketh not her own, is not easily provoked, thinketh no evil; rejoiceth not in iniquity, but rejoiceth in the truth; beareth all things, believeth all things, hopeth all things, endureth all things.

Love never faileth.

Self-Love

Self-love is impatient and uncharitable, and is a mass of jealousy; it keeps all its goods in the shop window, and cherishes inflated ideas of its own importance. Self-love has little consideration for others, is always out for "Number One"; it is touchy and highly critical of other people's conduct. Self-love has a secret sympathy with sin, and is always rather scared of the plain truth. It must never be put upon, it is suspicious and cynical and has little power of endurance.

Self-love soon tires of doing good.

If we are honest, we can easily see how much of the second definition there is in ourselves, and how that sort of spirit spoils relationships, whether between the partners of a marriage, the members of a family or group of people, or between nations. What a different world it would be if life were lived in the spirit of the first quotation, the spirit of true love!

The religion of Jesus Christ calls for a definite denial of the desires and impulses of the self-love that is in all of us, and a willingness to be guided and inspired by the power of true, not sentimental, love. Christians believe, and have proved, that God gives the ability to effect the change-over, once the decision to be done with self-love is sincerely made. We all have the power to love, and in our own hands lies the decision as to whether we turn that power in upon ourselves or give it to God and our fellow men.

21

"MY PAST HAS CAUGHT UP WITH ME"

It's just too bad, isn't it, when your past catches up with you? The unpleasant things you thought were safely dead and buried come to life and make you feel pretty cheap. It's apt to happen when we can't get off to sleep, or we are getting over the flu, or are just plain miserable.

Of course, some tough people never let this happen, or so they say. They've got the past properly buttoned up, and even if they've let down a friend or spoiled the niceness of a nice girl or sold someone a pup, it never comes between them and their sleep.

It's a great gift, this power of forgetting, and telling conscience where it gets off. You get much more peace of mind than our forefathers, who always seemed to be worrying about whether their sins were forgiven and whether they were safe for heaven. It used to be a matter of forgiving, now it's a matter of forgetting.

The happiest man is the man with the worst memory.

But suppose forgetting isn't enough. Suppose the past really has the power of catching up with us? Then the chap who thinks he's got the whole thing well under control is really living in a fool's paradise. He's holding down the memory of all the rotten things he's done, yes, but what happens when he can't do that any longer—when he dies, for instance?

Most people have a certain respect for the teaching of Jesus Christ, and one of the alarming things he said about the real world that is to follow this present set up is that "there is nothing hid that shall not be known" (Mark 4:22). It's easy enough to hide and pretend and get a cheap laugh here, but what about *there,* where there isn't a scrap of cover and your convenient powers of forgetting have disappeared?

What it boils down to is this. There are two quite different ways of dealing with the rotten things we've done. We can either "forget" them, which is like chucking all the rubbish into a cupboard and hoping the door won't burst open. Or we can have them acknowledged, apologized for, and forgiven—which is like having the cupboard clean and fresh and tidy.

Anyone, especially if he has a defective conscience, can "forget." Only God has the right, and the ability, to forgive—to delouse and disinfect the rottenness, and give enough impetus for a fresh start.

Being forgiven isn't morbid; it's just common sense.

22

"NO! NO! A THOUSAND TIMES NO!"

MANY PEOPLE LOOK UPON THE CHRISTIAN RELIgion as a very negative affair, consisting of a lot of "Thou shalt nots," and certainly including "Thou shalt not have a good time!"

This is partly the fault of some narrow-minded religious people (who certainly ought to know better), and partly because very few men and women trouble to find out what Jesus Christ himself really said, and was.

Consider, for instance, these facts about him, which you can verify yourself from your New Testament:

(1) So far from wanting people's lives to be anemic and negative, he said that he had come to bring them more life than they had ever known before (John 10:10).

"No! No! A Thousand Times No!"

(2) So far from being a kill-joy and puritan, he enjoyed the good things of life, and gained from religious people the reputation of being too fond of good food and the bottle (Luke 7:34).

(3) So far from adopting a "holier-than-thou" attitude, he loved all kinds of people (though he could be shatteringly rude to hypocrites, religious or otherwise), and thus got a name for keeping low company (Luke 15:2).

Life to Jesus Christ seems to have been the very opposite of a negative affair. He was positive, courageous, cheerful, and assured. He only insisted on one "No," and that is the "No" a man must say to his own love of himself before he can begin to learn what real positive living can be (Luke 9:23).

This is really only common sense if we think about it, for it is obvious that almost all the things which make life miserable for us or for other people spring from the root of self-love.

Look at it another way. We all have a certain amount of "love" in our make-up. This we can either turn in upon ourselves, which sooner or later means misery and loneliness and frustration, or we can deliberately deny this tendency and allow that love to go out toward God and other people, which will mean joy and satisfaction.

Every sin that ever was springs from that love turned in upon the self, and every bit of true happiness arises from love given away to someone else.

The trouble is that some people deny their love to themselves but never give it to anyone else. If we do that, we may think ourselves "holy," but we shall become narrow-minded nuisances to other people!

Christianity is emphatically *not* a religion of "A Thousand Times No!" The real Christian faces life positively and thoroughly enjoys everything that is good. But he has to keep on saying "No" to his self-love. This is not as easy as it sounds, but the Spirit of Jesus Christ is readily available to help him to make this denial, as every true Christian knows.

23

HE'S WONDERFUL, ISN'T HE?

EVERYBODY, UNLESS HE HAPPENS TO BE VERY self-centered, worships something or somebody—it's part of human nature. For some poor lonely old soul it may be only the cat or the canary, for a great many people it is a film star, a singer, an expert at some sport or other, or to a small minority some difficult but exquisite music on the program of a great pianist, which calls forth admiration, enthusiasm, and love.

It is very much this sort of thing that Christians mean when they talk about "worshiping" God. They mean that they have found Someone who is so lovable and wonderful and magnificent that he has touched the springs of worship in them far more powerfully and deeply than any human

Is God at Home?

being ever could and they simply want to worship him.

Naturally this seems nonsense to people who have little or no idea of what God is really like. If at the back of your mind you are thinking of God as a Spoil-sport or a Super Detective, the last thing in the world you'll want to do is to worship him. And if you have no more idea of God in your mind than you had when you were a small child, you haven't got anyone *big* enough to call forth your admiration, respect, and enthusiasm. You will no more want to worship the old childhood's idea of God than you nowadays want to play with the toys that were such a thrill to you when you were a child. You can't possibly want to worship in the Christian sense until you've seen how vast and wise, and yet how unbelievably generous and lovable, God really is.

But when you've got a grown-up idea of God, when you've seen that all the mystery and beauty in the world, all the "niceness" and kindness and humor that you love and admire in people, really come from God, you may quite possibly see what a wonderful Person he is. If you do, you'll want to worship.

And you'll want to worship more still if you

He's Wonderful, Isn't He?

accept this basic truth of Christianity—that God actually "focused himself" in a human being, whom we know by the name of Jesus Christ. If you really see that God is not only vast and immensely complex wisdom; not only the blazing Source of all truth and beauty; but is also very fond of us, so fond that he was willing to accept the limitations of being a human being, you can't help worshiping. Quietly and simply and without any fuss he came down to where we are so that he might help us rise to where he is. It meant for him a good deal of trouble and opposition, and in the end he (who was God, remember) accepted execution as a criminal—to show how far his love for us would go, and to bridge the gulf between himself and us. Once it dawns upon you what sort of God that means we have to deal with, you can hardly avoid saying, "Well, if he's *like that...*, I'd like to tell him, I'd like to *worship* him."

24

THE DUMB BLONDE

"OF COURSE," SAID THE FAT MAN, LEANING against the bar, "I like dumb blondes. In fact," he went on, pushing his glass across for a refill, "the dumber they are, the better I like 'em." There was a murmur of agreement.

The Fat Man might have gone a bit further. What he would really like would be a race of glamorous blondes, altogether charming and attractive, who would give him all the pleasure and thrill he wanted without his ever having to think that they might have minds—or even souls. He really wants his females to be living *things,* but not real people. And of course his attitude produces the female reply to that sort of thing—the gold digger.

Most of the miseries of this world are caused by this habit—treating other people as things, not

The Dumb Blonde

people. The employer who uses his employees as machines, the parent who regards his children as his own possessions, the young people who treat their home as simply a cheap hotel, the attractive girl who looks at all men as mere tributes to her sex appeal—they're all doing the same thing, trying to use people as things instead of recognizing them as people.

Of course it's a vicious circle. The Fat Man produces the gold digger, the inhuman employer produces the clock watcher, the possessive parent the thankless child, and so on *ad infinitum*. The world is full of it.

What is obviously wanted is a new spirit, something that will make people see one another and treat one another as people who matter, instead of exploiting them as things to be made use of.

Jesus Christ taught that this could be done if men would do two simple, though difficult, things.

First, recognize that there is a God who is equally the Father of everyone, Fat Man, blonde, parent, employer, employee, and all the rest, and give him a wholehearted loyalty.

Secondly, treat other people exactly as you would wish to be treated yourself—in other words, love your neighbor as yourself. Further, he said that

Is God at Home?

the Spirit to effect this change is immediately available to those who mean business.

A few have tried these two rules and they work. *How about you? Are other people just things to you, or are they fellow beings with the same Father?*

25

WHY SHOULD I SUPPORT THE CHURCH?

WELL, WHY SHOULD YOU SUPPORT THE CHURCH? The answer lies in whether you think the churches are filling a worth-while place in modern life. Obviously if you think that there are no such things as spiritual values and that there is no God to be worshiped; that there is no point in maintaining men to visit the sick, to cheer the lonely and depressed, and to give kindly and disinterested advice over life's many problems, then you won't give a cent to the Church, and you wouldn't shed a tear if all the churches in the land had to be closed through lack of support.

Yet there are many people who, though they rarely enter a church, would be extremely sorry to see them disappear from the pattern of our national life. Somehow they expect the church to be *there* and a clergyman or a minister to be available for their needs, if and when required. Indeed, such people are quite shocked when a church has to be closed through lack of money or man power, and are not slow to complain that "nobody ever visits them."

If we mean by "the Church" those who believe in and try to follow Jesus Christ, then it can never be destroyed, even if it has no financial support and even if it is bitterly persecuted. History proves this. But if you mean by "the Church" your particular church, with its ministry, its organizations, and its influence on the community, then that Church could very easily come to an end through sheer lack of support.

It is easy to moan about empty churches, particularly if we do nothing to fill them! It is easy to complain about depressed clergy and ministers, but the very reason why many of them grow depressed and depressing is because they do not get the backing of the men of good will who do at heart value what the Church stands for! It is easy to say that the country is going to the dogs, but how can the Church exert its proper influence if it is hamstrung by lack of support from so many people who care about an honest and decent life?

We don't need to be Jeremiahs to see that this is a materialistic age which is rapidly exhausting the spiritual capital of the past. Every church and chapel in the land is a natural rallying point for those who do believe that there is a spiritual meaning in life, and that there is a God who loves and cares what happens to us men. Don't stay outside and criticize; *come in and help!*

26

MEN UNDER RECONSTRUCTION

THERE ARE SOME PEOPLE WHO THINK THAT THOSE who go to church and support its activities consider themselves superior to the general run of mankind. Consequently, when the folk who are outside the Church are approached and urged to come inside, they're nearly always ready with some such remark as, "I'm quite as good as so-and-so"—so-and-so being a regular churchgoer.

It is high time this business was straightened out. In the first place it is nonsensical to say that church people for the most part think that they're any *better* than the people outside the Church; with very few exceptions they think nothing of the kind. It is in fact because they know that they're very far from good, and would like to be better

Men Under Reconstruction

men and women, that they seek the help of God in worship and prayer. This makes such a difference to their daily lives that they naturally want other people to come in and share what they have found so valuable. Sometimes this looks to the non-churchgoer like a "holier-than-thou" attitude. But it is really nothing of the kind.

Christians are in fact men and women "under reconstruction." Through contact with the live Spirit of the live God, they have come to see that inwardly their lives are a bit of a mess and that, with nothing but their own resources to draw upon, there is very little they can do about it.

This discovery about themselves is not nearly so gloomy and morbid as it may appear, for God does not wish men to remain groveling in their sins, still less brooding about them. He meets all men who see this need with something that they could never earn, full reconciliation with himself. But of course he does not leave them there, wonderful though it is to know that there is nothing on earth between you and the love of God. No, he proceeds, where men invite him to do so, to introduce his personality into their personalities, his Spirit into their spirits. Wherever God is genuinely invited to enter a human personality, he

Is God at Home?

—there is one side of life where he often hasn't grown up at all. In the realm of religion—that is, in his relationship with God—he has often made no progress at all with his adult mind. If he thinks about religion at all, it is in much the same terms that he used when he was at Sunday school. That is why a whole lot of people, quite grown-up in other ways, are prepared to write off the Christian religion as "kids' stuff."

Sometimes when a friend of ours seems to be hesitating about taking the adult line of action, we say, "Be your age, brother!" and that's quite often effective. But isn't it time that a great many people had the same thing said to them over the matter of the Christian religion? Most of them have never read the New Testament, for example, with their adult minds, or read a word of what really first-class brains like Dorothy Sayers or C. S. Lewis have to say about what they have come to believe is true. They are airily dismissing as "kids' stuff" something to which they've never given their grown-up attention at all. Yet surely, if we want to see any point or purpose in life, we might at least read and think for ourselves about this most important subject, and about that most astonishing claim, which the Man Jesus made, to be God in human form.

Be your age, brothers! This Christianity business is not really kids' stuff at all. It's much more like dynamite. Read for yourself and see!

28

WHY DON'T YOU RELAX?

EVERYBODY NEEDS TO RELAX AT SOME TIME OR ANother, and any doctor would tell you that to be able to relax your body and your mind completely is wonderfully refreshing to the whole system. But quite a lot of people, if the truth were told, find it very difficult to relax *inside themselves.*

Some people are afraid to relax because the moment they do so, all sorts of fears and anxieties crowd into their minds so that, in spite of all the armchairs and cushions, they're not really relaxed inside. Consequently, they plunge into their work in order to "forget" all the unpleasant bogeys of the mind.

Other people can relax to a large extent so long as they're with their friends, but when they're by themselves, they are very far from being relaxed and peaceful. People like this, though they probably don't admit it even to themselves, are really afraid of being alone with their own thoughts.

There is nothing new about this problem of relaxation, and the religion of Jesus Christ offers a practical and realistic way out. It diagnoses the trouble, and gives the solution, rather like this:

(1) Most people are not at peace with God or with their fellow men. Since none of us can undo the past, the Christian faith prescribes accepting the forgiveness of God and living in love and charity with our neighbor. (This may mean a certain amount of apology and admitting that we were wrong, but it's well worth the pain and effort.)

(2) The Christian faith recognizes that human beings have a conflict within themselves, and it prescribes the accepting of God's own Spirit into our own personalities so that what we sometimes call our better self is enormously strengthened, and the "worse self" loses its power.

(3) The Christian faith prescribes an attitude of faith rather than of fear toward life. However much appearances may be against it, God is really and ultimately in charge. Consequently, once our personalities are honestly entrusted to God, we can be sure there is nothing in life or

Is God at Home?

death that can alter the fact that our lives are lived "in God." That makes for a deep inner peace.

(4) Inward peace is not merely the absence of outward worry and strain. What we need is a positive peace which will keep us calm and poised, even when outward things are dark and difficult. Here the Christian faith offers us a *gift*. Christ says, "My peace I leave with you, my peace I give unto you," [1] and those who accept this gift find that they do experience right inside themselves "the peace which passes understanding." [2]

The above is not theoretical but intensely practical, as thousands have proved. There is no real and deep relaxation outside the peace of God.

---

[1] John 14:27.
[2] Philippians 4:7.

29

HAVE YOU A SPLIT PERSONALITY?

MAYBE YOU'RE INCLINED TO SAY YES! BUT REALLY a "split personality" or schizophrenia—the sort of thing we sometimes see films about—is a serious mental disease and is fortunately pretty rare. In a real schizophrenic one half of the personality acts without knowing at all what the other half is doing, and it needs real expert help to cure that sort of condition.

But what most of us mean when we think we've got two personalities in us is that we've got a good side and a bad side. When we try to be good, there is a side of us which says, "Oh, why bother—why not just please yourself?" and when we try to do something that is bad, there is a side that makes us draw back or gives us an uncomfortable attack of conscience.

Is God at Home?

This sort of split personality is common to everybody, and it often makes people feel very muddled inside themselves. One of the earliest Christians, Paul, wrote nineteen centuries ago: "The good that I want to do I find I don't do and the evil that I don't really want to do I find I am always doing" (Romans 7:19), and that goes for a good many people today as well. Paul found there was a way out. But before we look at it, let us see what happens to most people. As they get a bit older, they work out a sort of compromise so that they're never really good and never really bad; and, although at times they feel more than a little fed-up and dissatisfied, they regard this unsatisfactory situation as "just one of those things." But Paul and millions of Christians since his day have found that there is a way out—you needn't always live at sixes and sevens with yourself. The way out he recommended was to put his confidence in Jesus Christ (who, by the way, is just as much alive now as he was in Paul's day) and accept the reinforcement of his Spirit into his own personality. Once Paul, or anybody else for that matter, does that, he finds that the real and good side is enormously strengthened. The other side doesn't cease to exist, but its power gradually diminishes, and the attractiveness of the "lower" way of life largely disappears.

Real Christians all over the world have not only found this true; they have found that it makes life much more happy and real and satisfying. It isn't really much fun to live life as two people, each quarreling with the other. But once you make the decision and accept the Spirit of Christ, you find yourself, sometimes quite suddenly, becoming all of a piece, with the whole personality moving in the same direction. That is why real Christians have a joy and a peace which the man who lives with a working compromise never knows.

30

IS GOD DEAD?

A LOT OF PEOPLE SEEM TO THINK SO. AFTER ALL, they say, God doesn't seem to do very much, and nobody ever sees him.

Strangely enough, Christians do believe, not that God is dead *but that he did once die*. Dorothy Sayers (whose excellent detective stories you've probably read) wrote an article for the *Radio Times* called "The Execution of God"! She was writing of course about the crucifixion of a fine, courageous young man called Jesus Christ, over nineteen hundred years ago.

Naturally you can shrug your shoulders and say that he was just another martyr for the truth, and that's all there is to it. But if you read what he said about himself, it isn't as simple as all that. For his own claim, you can see for yourself, was undoubtedly that he was God—God in human form. He was "scaled down," of course, to match the life of this planet, but none the less genuinely God and a real human being at the same time. If he was right—and a lot of people think he was—then you can't regard his death as no more than a nasty little incident that happened ages ago.

Try to think of it with an unbiased mind. It is an amazing situation. God decides to exhibit his character in a way that men can understand by a personal visit to this planet that he has made. When he does so, a few recognize him, after a time, for what he is. A few more realize that what he tells them about God and man and life and all the other important things has the ring of truth—he sounds like an expert speaking on his own subject. A good many more don't care much one way or the other, while a few bitterly resent his exposure of their pride and greed and hypocrisy. He is "the real thing"; they are not, and they know it. Consequently they become so blinded with fury that they engineer a judicial murder.

They succeed. They manage to get the Man who claimed to be God killed. Nothing exciting happens; there is no celestial rescue party at the last moment. After suffering agony, he dies.

It rather changes your view of God if you be-

Is God at Home?

lieve he experienced this, particularly if you accept his own view. This was that his death was necessary in order to expose the nature of sin and to build a bridge between man and God. For most people know, even though they cannot put it into words, that there is an unpleasant gulf between them and God, caused by their own and other people's sin and selfishness. It is because of this gulf that God often seems so far away, or even dead, and however hard we try, we cannot bridge it. All serious religions attempt a kind of bridgehead toward God, but only Christianity builds the bridge. Incredible as it may seem, the Man-become-God, though himself sinless, allowed himself to be caught up in the sin-suffering-death mechanism which haunts mankind, in order to bridge the gap. We might truly say that he took the rap for mankind.

Everybody, consciously or unconsciously, is trying "to put up a case" to justify his actions before God. But it doesn't work. However hard we try, sooner or later we are forced to the conclusion that there is nothing *we* can do to close the gap between the terrifying purity of God and the sinfulness of men.

But what we could never do, *God has in fact*

Is God Dead?

done. The Bible says, "God was in Christ, reconciling the world unto himself" (II Corinthians 5: 19). That remains just a beautiful thought until you accept it. But once you drop your own attempts to make yourself good enough to get into touch with God, and accept this tremendous act of reconciliation as something done for you personally, then the picture miraculously clears. Now you can see God, not as a terrifying Judge or absentee Power, but as Someone who came right down into the sweat and pain and squalor of human life to win you to himself. Millions of people have found that, once they drop their own pretensions and accept quite simply this forgiveness, God becomes real—he becomes your Friend and not your enemy.

That was and is the real point and purpose of the Cross. It happened a long time ago, but it shows for all time the kind of God we have to deal with —One who would go to that length to bring you into friendship with himself.

www.ingramcontent.com/pod-product-compliance
Lightning Source LLC
Chambersburg PA
CBHW071332190426
43193CB00041B/1683